TENE

CW00871990

Editorial Everest would like to thank you for purchasing this book. It has been created by an extensive and complete publishing team made up of photographers, illustrators and authors specialised in the field of tourism, together with our modern cartography department. Everest guarantees that the contents of this work were completely up to date at the time of going to press, and we would like to invite you to send us any information that helps us to improve our publications, so that we may always offer QUALITY TOURISM.

QUALITY
TOURISM
WITH
EVEREST

Please send your comments to:
Editorial Everest. Dpto. de Turismo
Apartado 339 – 24080 León (Spain)
Or e-mail them to us at turismo@everest.es

Editorial Management: Raquel López Varela

Editorial coordination: Eva María Fernández

Text: Graciliano Martín Fumero

Photographs: Oliviero Daidola, Paolo Tiengo
and Archivo Everest

Diagrams: Mercedes Fernández

Cover design: Alfredo Anievas

Digital image processing: David Aller

Cartography: Montserrat Gual
© Everest

Translated by EURO:TEXT

All rights reserved. No part of this book may be reproduced, stored in a retrieval system,
or transmitted, in any form or by any means, electronic, mechanical, photocopying, recording or
otherwise, without the prior written permission of the holders of the Copyright.
This book is sold subject to the condition that it shall not, by way of trade or otherwise, be lent,
re-sold, hired out, or otherwise circulate without the publisher´s prior consent.

SCOND EDITION
© EDITORIAL EVEREST, S. A.
Carretera León-La Coruña, km 5 – LEÓN
ISBN: 84-241-0217-7
Legal deposit: LE. 24-2005
Printed in Spain

EDITORIAL EVERGRÁFICAS, S. L.
Carretera León-La Coruña, km 5
LEÓN (Spain)

TENERIFE

TENERIFE

Set in the Atlantic, like a jewel in precious metal, the island lies in the immensity of the ocean.

Achinech, Nivaria, Echeide, Tener-Ife... a diversity of names to say it, and each one of which constitutes a chapter in its history leading up to its present name: Tenerife. The *Adelantado* (Governor) Don Alonso Fernández de Lugo and his host subjected it to the Crown of Castile on the 25th of July 1496.

It is the largest of the islands that make up the archipelago of the Canaries, having a surface area of 2,036 km^2 with a current population of over 685,000 inhabitants living in the thirty-one townships embraced by **El Teide,** the highest peak in Spain, which rests on its torso.

The variety in its climate makes it attractive and the contrasts to be seen in its geography make it an enigmatic, magical paradise bound in mystery. At its heart the island holds a great diversity of native flora and fauna.

The Santa Cruz Carnival.

Rising up to the north and south are extensive tourist resorts that provide the entertainment of visitors to the island, who are greeted everywhere by the hospitality and friendly nature of the local people. It is rich in artistic, historic and musical patrimony, in folklore and gastronomy; it successfully combines its indigenous elements with those that have been brought from beyond. Tenerife is a mixture of both the cosmopolitan and the authentic —the magical spell of silence and dreams, of peaceful thought beneath the wide firmament of the globe.

To the north-east, on the untamed, rugged, open peninsula of Anaga - at the foot of the southern slope of the Dorsal Cordillera, stands the capital of the island: the Very Loyal, Noble, Unconquered and Generous City of **Santa Cruz de Santiago de Tenerife,** main port and trade centre of the island. Its citizenry displays a normality that contrasts with the sight of the tourists who come to admire what this city, five hundred years after it was founded, has to offer them. Santa Cruz de Santiago de Tenerife, a little nervous at the prospect of such an important anniversary, hurriedly puts on its festive attire. Extending over an area of 136 km^2 with

a population of 202,237 inhabitants, the capital emporium stretches out rectangularly towards the south to take in new quarters. Near the sea, an inspiration for artists, lies the port: aged, scarred by a multitude of events, but always willing to welcome both visits and trade. The port is graced by noble surroundings like the *Plaza de España* with its **Monument to Those Who Fell for the Fatherland.** An infinity of streets lead to this zone of expansion, sprinkled with a multitude of shops and official buildings: the *Palacio del Cabildo Insular* (Palace of the Island Council), Post Office Building, etc.

And along these streets of old cobblestones which have fallen under the yoke of asphalt, one can admire monuments of a religious, artistic and economic nature such as the church *Nuestra Señora de la Conception* which dates from the end of the 15th century, the old Island or Civil Hospital which, built in neo-classical style, is now a museum, the Internal Revenue Delegation Building and, standing nearby, the Presidential Palace. All of these buildings stand along the tree-lined *Avenida Bravo Murillo.*

Stretching out from another corner of this beloved, charming city settled by emigrants is a second avenue: a fortified wall that has been witness to battles of past eras such as that of the defeat of the British Admiral Nelson off the coast of Añaza. Today this coast is called Anaga, and a small fort rises up on its slopes, keeping a constant vigil over the

Several examples of the island's cuisine.

View of the port of
Santa Cruz.

Almeida castle,
with the port in the
background.

Following double
page, general view
of Santa Cruz.

unpredictable ocean: the Almeida Fort.
The coastal road makes its way down
past a succession of buildings,
neighbourhoods and business premises
to the *San Andrés* port district. Here, set
among the cliffs, is the *Playa de las*

Teresitas, a beach with tinted-gold sand.
A breakwater holds back the arrogant
sea, subduing its inexhaustible might.
The scene is one of pleasure boats,
fishermen and people from the world of
affairs in search of a moment's leisure.

On venturing further northwards, along winding secluded roads that here and there afford splendid views, one comes across the foothills of the mountain range amidst a scenery of rocky terrain, cliffs and coves. Rugged paths lead us on to a village, **Taganana,** a gateway back to times when life was simpler, lying far away from the constant hustle and bustle of the city, on a site cut out of the mountains by the forces of erosion. Taganana jealously guards a church which is dedicated to *Nuestra Señora de las Nieves* and which conserves a Flemish triptych from the second third of the 16th century in its interior. We take to the road again for our return in the hope of discovering new places, and stop for a while at the oldest town on Tenerife: **San Cristóbal de la Laguna.** From the late poet,

Pedro García Cabrera, I take these verses to reflect the sentiments that this University Town, the town of the Governors awakens in all who decide to take a rest here from their arduous journey: 'Grant me the honour of taking you under my wing / city in whose streets the blood in my veins / has throbbed like nightingale song; / Oh city that rises to face / the freedom of the horizon'. This is a noble, cultured, aged city with a distinguished bearing where silence blindly walks, bent double, at the mercy of the sun's charity. The *Torre de la Concepción* watches over the Spanish Renaissance church of the same name and has borne witness to many a violent struggle… And, further down lies the Cathedral, stronghold and strongbox, confessional and museum of great architectural, pictorial and sculptural value.

View of Taganana.

Tower of la Laguna Cathedral. ▶

Roques de Taganana.

LA LAGUNA

Aguere, the muse, the first capital, rests on *La Vega* (The Fertile Plain) where the days, in chorus and tinted with fog, play at the Witches' Sabbath. Founded in 1496, this town was the seat of the first Island Council, the origin of all the statutory provisions and the institution in which the activities of all the organs of the central administration were carried out. With an extension of 102.05 km^2 and 112,917 inhabitants, the City of the *Adelantados* has quickly opened out to embrace the bustle of modern culture, a culture in which words are seen to crystallize and fall from conversation, finally coming to rest on the cobble stones that have been worn down as a result of so much traffic. La Laguna is an episcopal see, rich in world heritage and aristocratic in its bearing. The old urban centre constitutes a tapestry of what was typical of colonialism during the period of its foundation. San Cristóbal also has been a university town since 1744, thanks to the Augustinian Order. In 1817 the first building of the institution of learning was built, and it received the name of San Fernando. In 1927 it received the rank and distinction of university. Its campus: A place of joy and disappointment, conspiracies and secret loves, the embrace of cultures. In summer, La Laguna plays host to pilgrimages and celebrations of folklore; it becomes a cosmopolitan crossroads, the backcloth for both intellectual discussion and religious processions…

San Cristóbal de La Laguna holds out a friendly hand to the lands over the seas that share its own language.

Tacoronte, land of local colour, a carousel of festivities and devotion. This is a town that boasts many places of worship, such as the Church of *Santa Catalina* and that of *El Cristo de los Dolores,* a town which openly shows its faith on the feast of Corpus Christi. It also turns out in disguise on the occasion of its *Piñata Chica* and 'steals' wines from the god Bacchus in order to offer them at the *Alhóndiga,* the famous former corn exchange. And as one descends along the road to Tacoronte, which winds its way down to the rugged coast, one reaches another township: El Sauzal. After the conquest, the Governor Alonso Fernández distributed the island's land and water among his forces, thus ensuring the agricultural prosperity of the cereal covered slopes of the island. This town is endowed with a number of springs and therefore features land suited to the cultivation of crops. To give thanks for these blessings, Alonso Fernández de Lugo ordered the construction of a hermitage dedicated to the *Virgen de Los Ángeles* (Our Lady of the Angels). The historical relevance of El Sauzal dates from the end of the 16th century when it was the island's administrative and political centre for a time, although subsequently it was to

10

The Casa de Carta Ethnological Museum in Tacoronte.

Views of the
Lago Martiánez
complex in
Puerto de la Cruz.

be decimated by the so called 'London Plague'. However, El Sauzal was once also home to an important aborigine settlement, which was located in the Cabrera Ravine. Now the town has the air of a luxuriant garden and its Church of San Pedro —which dates from the 16th century and contains such riches as the statue of the Baby Jesus from the 17th century or its silver tabernacle— invites one to indulge in contemplation. El Sauzal is witness to the constant movement on its sea and coast. On the way to Puerto de la Cruz, one perceives yet another town, looking like a beauty spot on the skin of this island: **La Matanza de Acentejo.** Lying to the north, this medium-sized town stretches out over 14.11 km² and has 6,172 inhabitants. It is set in an area renowned for its wine production. Indeed, the local wines are known to inspire songs and kindle dreams. La Matanza de Acentejo is the historic site of sorrowful events which have given it its name (The Slaughter of Acentejo). In its jagged ravines important battles were fought in which victory belonged to the Guanches, the island's aborigines, who decimated the Governor's troops in 1494, thus converting the San Antonio Ravine into both battlefield and cemetery. This is the site of festivals in honour of St. Anthony the Abbot, occurring shortly after Christmastide, where the tradition is

Following double page,
the Parrot Park
in Puerto de la Cruz.

the *Baile del Niño* (Dance of the Child) to the music of the *tajaraste* in the sublime Parish Church of El Salvador.
Still in the Acentejo area, **La Victoria de Acentejo,** the revenge of conquerors on the guanches: famed for its folklore, gastronomy and handicrafts, this unique town is silhouetted against the backcloth of the ocean. And beside the sea: **Puerto de la Cruz,** the old port of La Orotava. Travellers like to take a break at this cosmopolitan, tourist-oriented resort. Among the attractions here are *Loro Parque* (Parrot Park), Mariánez Lake, *Castillo de San Felipe* (San Felipe Castle) and the Botanical Garden, which shelters a multitude of flowers from the whole world. It was founded in 1788 during the reign of Carlos III and laid out by Don Alonso de Nava y Grimón, Marquis of Villanueva del Prado. This historic town was emancipated from the Villa of La Oratava by Royal Warrant on the 28th of November 1648, under the government of King Philip IV. Its first mayor was Don Antonio de Franchy y Fonte del Castillo. Puerto de la Cruz celebrates a wide range of festivities. On the feast day of St. John, animals are taken to the sea to benefit from its healing waters; on that of St. Andrew the *'Jura de la Pipa'* (Oath of the Pipe) is sworn; St. Lucia´s day and many other occasions are also observed…

prosperous economy brought it to jurisdictional emancipation from La Laguna in the year 1648.

La Orotava conserves streets in which constructions of great value rise up; buildings which date from the 17th and 18th centuries, such as the House of the Balconies, the House of the Medina Family, and those of the Monteverdes, the Lercaros…

The Church of the Immaculate Conception, dating from the second half of the 18th century, was constructed by the architects Diego Nicolás and Ventura Rodríguez with a Baroque façade and

14

At the heart of the island, where the volcano stands between hills and valleys, lies **La Orotava,** another town of *Nivaria.* This is Taoro, an emerald green area dotted with noble homes; this is the land of *Bentenuhya,* of its adopted son Humboldt. Here we also find the Teide National Park.

The town of La Orotava is an historical relic, whose houses in the old quarter date from the beginning of the colonisation at the end of the conquest. To be seen here are noble buildings that once belonged to the Governor's troops and which are referred to as 'Twelve Houses'. Its flourishing agriculture and

Rococo elements and has been declared a National Monument. Among the works of sacred art it holds are its three altarpieces, a statue of St. Peter by Estévez, one of the Sorrowful Mother and another of St. John the Evangelist by Luján. There are also frescos by Cristóbal Hernández de Quintana and Gaspar de Quevedo.

La Orotava, a backstitch in an enigmatic valley, brings together a diversity of customs and traditions which link it with other lands and cultures, forming a rainbow of hope.

This high flat land constitutes a great garden with a wealth of different plants

View of the historical quarter of La Orotava.

Festival time in La Orotava.

The exterior of the House of Los Balcones.

and crops. It is verdant, with forests of lauriselva, of pines, of broom and laburnum on its peaks, perfuming the mists that roll down from the mountain to the town.

La Orotava is Aguamansa, Benijos, La Florida, Pinoleris, the Ravine of *La Madre* or of Pedro Gil, it is La Caldera, El Rincón, El Bollullo.

La Orotava is also its *bananera* or banana industry, constantly transforming bananas into liquors and jams. La Orotava also boasts a number of watermills, true works of art transporting the liquid element to all parts, satisfying needs, making dreams come true.

This town is synonymous with crafts and festivities. Here the visitor comes across artisans who do openwork, embroidery, macramé, and work with the pole, wood, leather... Local pilgrimages take place on the Feasts of *San Isidro* and *Santa María de la Cabeza;* on such occasions the whole town is decked out in the time-honoured manner and the most typical island dress is worn, all in keeping with the traditional folklore.

La Orotava is also the gardens at the Santa Clara Monastery, popularly known as the 'Off-shoot of the Botanical Garden', where one can contemplate plant species from three

continents: cedars, dracenas and palms grow next to bamboo, sambucus, caneyus and coffee trees; whilst thorn-apples and ferns combine harmoniously with hydrangeas, lantanas and wisteria, water lilies, papyruses, araucarias, magnolias... an authentic breath from nature's lungs which perfumes and oxygenates a good part of this valley sunk in a thousand memories. Focal point of Corpus Christi celebrations, La Orotava carpets its streets with art, mixing coloured earth with reeds and flower petals to obtain religious images.

El Teide National Park.

♦ Floral floor-coverings opposite the City Hall during the festival of La Orotava.

La Orotava is of course also famous for its **Teide National Park,** which, before being established as such by decree on 22nd January 1954, had formerly served as pasture land for the indigenous people's livestock. We enter the exotic paradise of *Las Cañadas,* mysterious and impressive, by the Aguamansa roads. The park occupies an area of 135 km², and begins at an altitude of 2,000 metres. It is composed of a succession of almost vertical rock walls and lava cones, called *circos*. In the centre of this rises the peak of El Teide, standing 3,718 metres high. There is a refuge shelter and a funicular goes up to the summit. The surrounding hills, such as that of Guajara, and the *Montaña Blanca* (White Mountain) crater and the Ucanca plateau have provided the scene for many legends... The different hues of the various superimposed layers of lava flow create a multicoloured landscape which is called *Los Azulejos* (The Decorated Tiles). These are lands of perennial silence that have their very own endemic vegetation: broom, laburnum, cedars, straw grass, wallflowers, teide violets, tajinaste —a chromatic explosion that stands out from the grey and ochre of the ground to which it is wed. At *Las*

Cañadas the *Parador Nacional de Turismo* (State owned and operated tourist hotel) provides a welcome rest for those tired after a hard day's walk. Las Cañadas is also the name of the local cemetery, a place for pleasant, peaceful rest. From up on high the mist rolls down, eventually to turn into seaspray, and shrouds the venerable mountain in its very best gown, as if protecting its immaculate body.

EL TEIDE

El Teide, which has an altitude of 3,718 m., is found within the township of La Orotava. According to geologists, its genesis dates back 600,000 years and it would seem its formation has not been concluded yet, since in the year 1798 there was an eruption and one can still see fumaroles. The mountain lies right in the middle of *Las Cañadas*. In the words of Leoncio Alfonso: 'What we have before us here is the most striking and spectacular formation of the island, one which rises 1,700 metres from the base and is formed by a double volcano'. It is believed that the double cone, called *Pico Viejo* (Old Peak) was created some 2,000 years ago.

Turning away from this rocky fortress, we can also make out valleys and plains which give the area an enigmatic air. The climate of the Teide National Park is the similar to that found on subtropical high mountains. Being situated above the zone of inversion of the Trade Winds, it has higher temperatures and is drier. As far as its vegetation is concerned, its surface is sprinkled with abundant indigenous plants, an example being the broom. The Peak of El Teide,

god of forbears who invoked good omens, is ready to act as a stage for one´s most exalted thoughts.
Lying within the area of Taoro there is another township: **Los Realejos.** Having a wide range of geographical features, it is lieterally scarred with ravines. La Rambla and Hondo, where antagonistic echoes add to the music of water or the whistle of the wind. Here, mountainous terrain is seen to merge into hills which in turn roll down to the sea. At dusk the

Three views of the National Park.

El Roque Chinchado with the Teide in the background. ▶

pine covered heights are alive with the wild melodies of nature. Finally there is the coast, combining sighs with dawns, bringing memories home in the early mornings of summer. All along the coast lie a number of tourist resorts: La Romántica and Rambla de Castro.

But Los Realejos is no stranger to the island's history either, because the Governor's troops camped on its lands before setting out to do battle with the insurgent Guanches that remained in the area. Los Realejos is also the grave of the Guanche prince Bentor, who hurled himself from the heights of Tigaiga. It has also become renowned due to the great historian and scholar, José Viera y Clavijo. Los Realejos is a sanctuary of faith, of local colour, of patrimony. Throughout history it has been the possession of princes and the property of Governor Alonso Fernández de Lugo. Los Realejos lies in a flourishing valley that is rich in legends.

Las Cañadas del Teide
National Parador Hotel. ▶

Las Cañadas del Teide National Park.

ICOD DE LOS VINOS

Icod de los Vinos and the millennial drago tree.

The lands of Bentenuhya lead us on past a succession of new spots such as La Guancha and San Juan de la Rambla to another area of the island: Icod de los Vinos. Icod or *Benico den de Chincanairo* is a landscape marked by pronounced steep slopes and plains, one that features mountain terrain cleft by ravines and a rugged coastline bordered by sheer cliffs. It also has a small bay that serves both as a harbour and a beach: San Marcos. Here, the slow passing of time and the sea have conspired to give new forms to the lava and to create this treasure chest of ever-changing fortunes. Black sands weave sea foam into scarves of history which lend warmth to the air.

Icod is synonymous with its dragon tree, on which the passing of centuries seems to weigh heavily, weary as it is of so many mundane episodes and the epic procession of anonymous faces that file past it in the *Plaza de Lorenzo Cáceres.* This is a festive, devout, ancestral *Benico den,* where the night air dances to the sound of the *tajaraste.*

And from the Icod of Emeterio Gutiérrez Albelo we continue on our way to the Daute area or the region of Teno where,

rising up on a hill in the shape of a shell, is the township of **Garachico.**

Here lies the Cove of Interián, which at the conclusion of the conquest belonged to a number of Genoese families —Cristóbal de Ponte, Mateo Viña, Agustín and Pantaleón Italiano, Pedro de Interián, Fabián Viña— and which remains a reminder of the former Garachico which lies beneath the lava flows provoked by

Tower of the church of San Marcos, in Icod.

the eruption of the Montañas Negras (Black Mountains) in 1706. Both the town and the port are of great architectural wealth. There is the Castle of *San Miguel,* from the 16th century, whose artistic interest is based on the purpose for which it was intended… It is a thick walled fortification featuring turrets at the corners, an alarm bell tower to warn of the approaching foe, loopholes and merlons crowning the walls and heraldic arms over the principal entrance. The building has recently been restored and fitted out to serve as an exhibition hall. Other monuments of Garachico worthy of mention are the Church of *Santa Ana,* convent of the Order of the Immaculate Conception, the churches of *Santo Domingo* and *San Francisco,* the 15th-century Church of *San Pedro de Daute,* the 17th-century Palace of the Counts of La Gomera, featuring a baroque façade, the houses of Lamero de Ponte… Garachico is also known for its *Puerta de Piedra,* in former times a busy gateway and today the scene of a park and poets' corner…

We spin atmospheres and we weave all that our eyes capture on the looms of our imaginations. We are still in Daute, down by the sea in the township of **Buenavista del Norte.** The ocean thrusts its might against the massive rocks and steeply rising cliffs from which silence plunges into the sea to drown in its roar and on

which new hopes are born. The ravine drowns its lament in the sea and, cleansed by the seaspray, it conceals its history in the deepest of its crevices. Heading inland from the ravine, we arrive at a typical country hamlet, a tourist attraction: Masca. **Masca** is an unequalled spot for those who desire to spend a few hours in contact with nature and at the same time admire traditional primitive architecture, an architecture which here is preserved in great purity. Its dwellings nestle atop a series of hillocks that seem to proudly contemplate the vertiginous, gaping hollows of the ravines. The gentle breeze caresses the branches of the orange and almond trees as the days slowly drift away; orange and lemon blossoms flourish against the steep slopes, and meanwhile the silent palm grove faithfully keeps watch. Masca, renowned for its ethnographical interest and its handicrafts, seems frozen in an age of legends. From Masca our tour takes us on to Las Portelas, a centre for traditional wickerwork goods.

22

BUENAVISTA

From the hamlets of the Buenavista area we now move on to the town itself, leaving behind us banana plantations and potato fields.

Here we see wide, straight streets lined with brilliant white houses hung with balconies in the island style.

Buenavista del Norte also boasts its own places of cultural interest. The Church of the *Virgen de los Remedios,* with architectural elements from the 16th century, jealously guards in its interior a statue of the Virgin of Remedies which also dates from the 16th century. In addition there is a statue of St. Francis, by Alonso Cano, and another of St. Joseph. Canary and American goldsmithery also form part of the town´s legacy.

In October Buenavista takes on a festive atmosphere in celebration of its patron saint, who is said to have performed a miracle to free the town of the plague of locusts that occurred in 1659.

The carved image of the saint that is carried through the streets in the processions is decorated with gold and silver orchids brought here by emigrants from Venezuela, the so-called *eighth island* of the Canaries. This traditional festivity is also popularly known as the 'Feast of the Cicada'.

Buenavista del Norte forms part of the so-called *Isla Baja* or Lower Island and is predominantly a comunity of farm labourers and craftsmen. It brings together sentiments that help to serve progress, while banishing the secrets of its charm to the sea, so as not to fall into negligence or succumb ot irrational adventures.

Buenavista del Norte was once the town of the *Mencey* Caconamio, the favoured tagoror of Achaxucanac.

Turning our atention to the south of *Echeide,* we come across a valley and a plain near Ucanca: this is **Santiago del Teide.** An area once overrun by the flow of lava, it also features craggy terrain and sheer rock faces, and is cradled by the eternal mountains that surround it.

Watching out over this landscape are the peaks of Abeque, genuine outposts from times of silence… Santiago del Teide is Arguayo, Los Gigantes, and Puerto Santiago with its beach called *La Arena.* It is not lacking in historical interest. During his time as ruler of the town,

La Arena beach, in Puerto Santiago.

Below and following
double page,
different views of
Los Gigantes.

Don Fernando del Hoyo had a church built, dedicated to St. James. Subsequently, by means of a royal decree of 10th of May 1678, the church obtained the status of parish church and was given the name of *San Fernando Rey.*
These are thirsty lands carpeted with grapevines and *tagasastes,* the latter adding a dash of optimism to the otherwise sombre surroundings. They are lands that are encrusted in lava and are thus afforded noble protection.
Santiago del Teide is a coast seemingly visited by the gods, featuring Puerto Santiago and the sheer cliffs of Los Gigantes. Santiago is also the sea, stretching out into the distance, whose foam-capped waves are ploughed by fishing vessels and sailing yachts alike. Turning back from the unfathomable ocean and heading inland, we perceive a singular district rising up over a hillock, a balcony on which memories await the arrival of new hopes. This is **Tamaimo,** renowned for its lookout-point, the *Mirador de Lara.* So great is the activity of the local people that the town seemingly has no fixed working hours.

25

Barranco del Infierno (Hell's Ravine).

SANTIAGO DEL TEIDE

A shady mount, divorced from time, which ponders the trees that die in the quiet of the days. A mount of silence, a cemetery of history, where life has spun innumerable episodes.

Here we see the hills of Abeque and Bolicos; the mountains of Gala and of Bilma, a scene of parched *malpais* or rough lava-covered terrain, the result of battles lost in the struggle against the Chinyero Volcano. An unfaithful mountain, forever ready to receive the loving embrace of the mist; heights that enclose a valley affording shelter for the life forms.

A mountain peak constantly yearning to be at the heart of *Nivaria*, whispering to El Teide in the hope of dispelling its century-old sadness, longing for the sentiments of the indigenous peoples that once dwelt in Arguayo. A mount that stretches down into the sea, to the ocean that clads it each day in saltpetre, in preparartion for its departure into the unknown.

Mount Santiago del Teide becomes a fortress and gives refuge to the authentic feelings of the souls who yearn for progress.

Still in the region of Isora, we carry on to another of its townships: **Adeje.**

The extensive erosion undergone by this area has lent its inland terrain a wide range of striking features, such as the rock formations of El Conde, Imoque and Abinque or the *Barranco del Infierno* (Hell´s Ravine), all of which afford the visitor stretches of memorable scenery. Its coastline is marked by soaring cliffs and a series of beaches —such as those of *Las Américas, Callao Salvaje* or *Playa Paraíso*— that have become a focal point of the island´s booming tourism.

Formerly covered with tomato plants and banana plantations that in time would be sacrificed in the march of progress, today these lands have given rise to

Above, El Médano; below, Callao Salvaje. ▸

Typical Arguayo pottery.

Above and opposite page, different views of Las Américas Beach.

countless estates that accommodate tourists from all corners of the world. Moreover, a whole succession of other resorts are seen to line the coast, such as that of **Torviscas,** itself a small town that constitutes a microcosm of numerous cultures, most of which originate in Europe. Due to its climate and the cosmopolitan atmosphere one breathes, many are the outsiders who have abandoned their own countries to come to these shores, eminently touristic in nature, and combine their customs with the new ones they encounter in their new surroundings and which they make their own. All the comforts and amenities which one could wish to enjoy are within easy reach here; there is no need to venture out of the town. The architecture of the town blends harmoniously with the local scenery, and together with the latter has attracted and captured the imaginations of restless foreigners, those tireless travellers forever in search of peace and quiet. From Torviscas we move on to **Playa de Las Américas,** a resort used by the people of Adeje and Arona alike. This is

◀ The Aqua-Park.

and houses harmoniously built with recreation facilities for the tourist. An exotic atmosphere is created by the local flora, which provides welcome oxygen for this resort of many languages.

Reefs, dikes and sea walls create a calm sea where sighs delve into the depths. Las Américas is also equipped with a sheltered harbour for sports craft: **Puerto Colón,** where row upon row of yachts and speedboats hold the promise of hours of entertainment out on the open sea, a sea which jealously guards its secrets, confessions or, simply, its feelings.

The streets of these tourist resorts form a network of straight lines. Long, wide promenades run along the shore and are lined by countless bars and shops. Many secluded corners, squares or open places featurs modern sculptures, that portray one or other heroic deed or historic personality, or simply reflect the atmosphere that a given site evokes.

Along these coasts of black or golden sands the sea lays down its head to rest, and every now and then is disturbed by a gentle breeze.

This is the coast of *Atguaxona* or Atbitocazpe, a reemergence of intentions and desires that once implied good fortune.

Previous double page, night view of Las Américas Beach.

the coast along which, in time gone, by Tenerfe the Great, King of the Menceyes, decided upon many of his projects designed for the good of his island. Here we find a diversity of coves for the enjoyment of bathers as well as a seemingly unending range of buildings

34

This page and opposite page, different views of Colón Harbour.

From the coastal territory of Adeje we move on to the elevated region of Abona and finally reach the township **Arona.** Arona is noted for its *Roque de Vento* and its mountains called Chijafe, Higara and Chineja, silent, soaring formations that exude solitude.

The Valley of San Lorenzo is an area marked by agricultural abundance, where banana trees and tomato plants coexist with cacti and a number of other indigenous plant species.

Historic Arona... whose Church of *San Antonio Abad,* built in the first half of the 17th century, received the honour of being raised to the rank of parish by Bishop Tavira in 1796. Within this church are found such artistic treasures as the statue of the *Cristo de la Salud* and an Immaculate Conception, both from the 18th century. There is also the coast of Arona which offers complexes like Los Cristianos, Costa del Silencio, Las Galletas, Ten Bel, Palm-mar, where the open sea is seen to come crashing onto the beaches, providing perfect conditions for windsurfers.

At arona we come across the sea port of **Los Cristianos,** from which people hurry on their way to the Columbine Island of La Gomera, a stream of immigrants in search of better fortune.

The lands awaiting us in the south of the island are arid and silent but can always count on the welcome presence of the wind. Travelling along the well-beaten tracks of this area, we come to a town that rises up in the middle of a valley. Before we arrive, however, we pass through El Escobonal, in the region of Agache, Lome de Mena, La medida or Chacona de Arriba, and stop a while at the *Don Martín* lookout point, from where we can admire the island landscape that stretches out before us. Finally, we make our way down to the town of **Güímar** which was born, according to the chronicles of the time, in the second half of the 16th century in the renowned neighbourhood of San Juan, in the proximity of the hermitage of the same name. Nearby we find the source of *El Río* and the *Barranco de Badajoz*.

On this page, view of the Arona area. Opposite page, San Lorenzo valley.

The Costa del Silencio (the Coast of Silence).

Los Cristianos beach.

Los Cristianos harbour.

Previous double page,
view of Vilaflor.

Festivities in
La Candelaria. ▶

◀ Views of Granadilla.

Above us, on a hill, lies another township: **Arafo,** whose peaks are covered with pine woods which descend over slopes and ravines. At the town's entrance there is a pine that stands, proud and defiant, as if guarding the chapel that shields a statue of Christ commonly referred to as *El Señor del Pino* (Lord of the Pine). The population of Arafo flourished with its sawmill. The town itself is set on farmland and pastures, the latter lying in the areas of Chivisaya and Afoña, the eternal guardians of the slopes of *El Gorgo.*

Candelaria is the last township in the region of Güimar. It covers an area of 49.52 km². Locate amidst rugged mountainous terrain, the town lies on a coast lined with sheer cliffs. Right from its very beginnings, Candelaria has been under the protection of the Blessed Virgin Mary, the patron saint of the Canary Islands. The original statue of the Virgin was lost in a landslide in 1826 which also destroyed the castle and the Dominican convent.

Our Lady of La Candelaria.

Basilica of La Candelaria
and statues of the
Menceyes Guanches.

Candelaria.
Church.

It is said that the origin of this town lies in the *Santa Ana* district which, rising up on a cliff, has evolved around the church of the same name. Many of the houses here are examples of traditional architecture.

The *Plaza de la Basílica* guarded by the *Menceyes* of the Guanches; other places of interest in the town are the neighbourhoods of *La Hoya* or *El Pozo*, along with *El Chinchorro* Beach, home of a long-standing fishing tradition.

Candelaria has a great deal to offer the tourist, both in the town itself and on its shores, at *Las Caletillas*. It also boasts a rich cultural heritage.

It is also an industrial town with a flourishing economy and leaves no stone unturned in its search for progress. Set in a region lying in a valley of adventure, it has a cosmopolitan atmosphere and is always striving to attain new goals in order to ensure its survival.

Future and past. Above, the astrophysical observatory below, Guanche mummies in the Santa Cruz museum.

Typical Tenerife architecture.